# THE UNFORTUNATE LAUNCH OF THE SPACE SHUTTLE CHALLENGER

US History Books for Kids

Children's American History

Speedy Publishing LLC

40 E. Main St. #1156

Newark, DE 19711

www.speedypublishing.com

Copyright 2017

The explosion of the space shuttle Challenger in 1986 was one of the worst disasters so far for the space missions of any country. Find out what happened, and why.

# A REUSABLE SPACE CRAFT

The National Aeronautics and Space Administration (NASA) wanted a reusable space craft that could carry, not just astronauts, but mini-laboratories and cargoes of satellites to launch into orbit. In 1976 they displayed the first model of a reusable space vehicle, the space shuttle.

DESERT TESTS LUNAR "RV"
NASA
NASA

SPACE SHUTTLE ATLANTIS

The space shuttle left the earth with the power of two huge rocket boosters and an external fuel tank. As the fuel tank got empty, the shuttle would discard it and the rockets, and continue into orbit as a wide-winged craft that could navigate space near earth, and also move through the atmosphere safely to bring its crew to a soft landing like a jet plane.

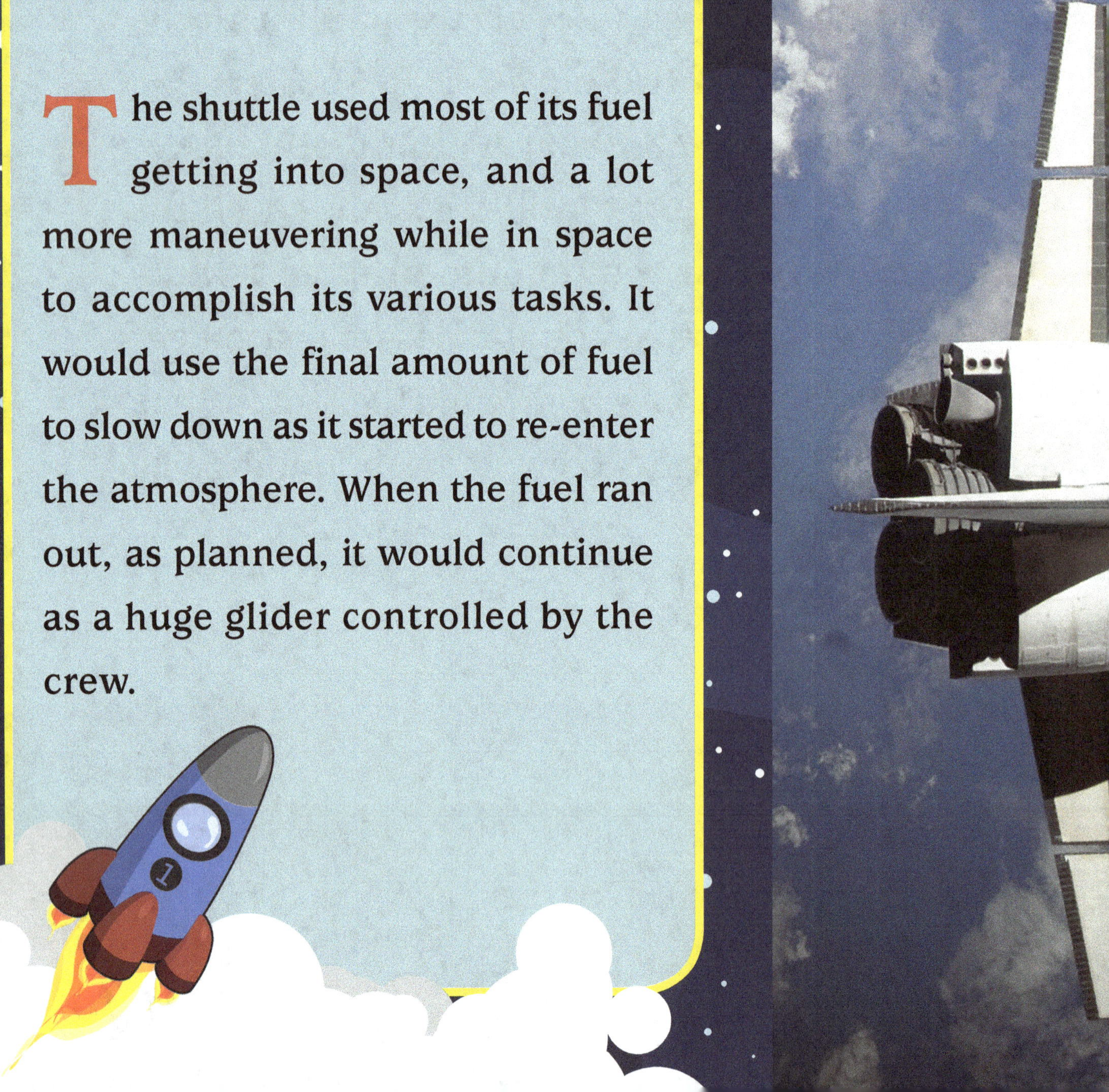

The shuttle used most of its fuel getting into space, and a lot more maneuvering while in space to accomplish its various tasks. It would use the final amount of fuel to slow down as it started to re-enter the atmosphere. When the fuel ran out, as planned, it would continue as a huge glider controlled by the crew.

SPACE SHUTTLE ENDEAVOUR IN ORBIT

## SPACE SHUTTLE COLUMBIA

The first operational shuttle, Columbia, made its first flight in 1981.

SPACE SHUTTLE CHALLENGER

The second shuttle, Challenger, made its first voyage in 1983.

# THE CHALLENGER'S CREW

By 1986, Challenger had completed nine missions. The next trip was scheduled for January 22, 1983, with a seven-member crew. They were:

- Mission Commander Dick Scobee
- Pilot Mike Smith
- Mission Specialists Judith Resnik, Ronald McNair, and Ellison Onizuka
- Payload Specialists Gregory Jarvis and Christa McAuliffe

**SPACE SHUTTLE CHALLENGER'S CREW**

SPACE SHUTTLE COLUMBIA'S CREW
BROWN CLARK CHAWLA ANDERSON RAMON
HUSBAND MCCOOL
STS 107

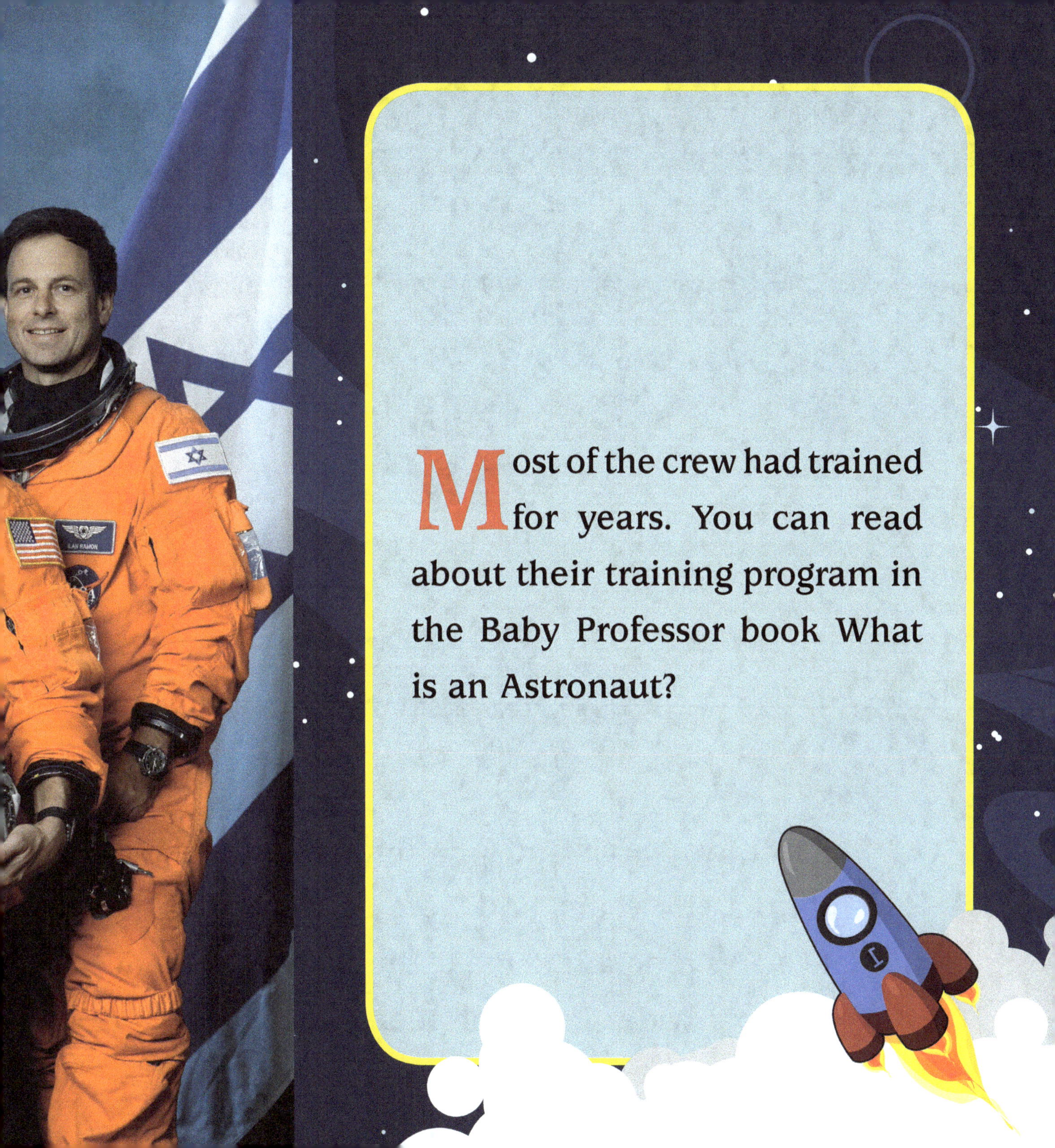

The last two, Jarvis and McAuliffe, had trained for months, not years, and were on the mission as part of NASA's program to make the space experience available to a wider range of people.

**J**arvis worked on advanced satellite designs for Hughes Aircraft, and McAuliffe was a high-school teacher from New Hampshire. She was due to be the first "ordinary American" to go into space, and that attracted a lot of interest across the country and around the world.

# THE LAUNCH AND WHAT HAPPENED

The launch of Challenger on its tenth mission was set for January 22, 1986, but NASA had to delay it for nearly a week, partly because of bad weather and partly so the ground crew could solve some technical issues.

**THE SPACE SHUTTLE CHALLENGER**

SPACE SHUTTLE CHALLENGER LAUNCHING

Finally, the launch was set for January 28, which was a very cold morning. Engineers warned their managers that some parts of the shuttle and its engines might not work well under cold conditions. These included the O-rings, rubber washers that sealed the joints of the booster rockets. The managers decided to go ahead anyway.

Late in the morning, Challenger lifted off its launch pad. A large crowd watched the space shuttle lift into the sky. But just over a minute into the mission, the plume of smoke from the engines split into two plumes. The shuttle, its rockets, and its fuel tank collapsed into pieces and fell into the Atlantic Ocean. Every member of the crew died.

CHALLENGER BROKE APART
AFTER LAUNCH IN 1986, KILLING
ALL CREW ON BOARD

**ROGERS COMMISSION MEMBERS ARRIVE
AT KENNEDY SPACE CENTER**

# THE ROGERS COMMISSION

President Ronald Reagan called together a group of experts to find out what had happened to the Challenger, and to recommend what NASA should do to prevent a similar accident in the future. The commission was headed by former Secretary of State William Rogers, and is generally known as the Rogers Commission. Astronauts Neil Armstrong and Sally Ride, and Chuck Yeager, a famous test pilot for jet planes, served on the commission.

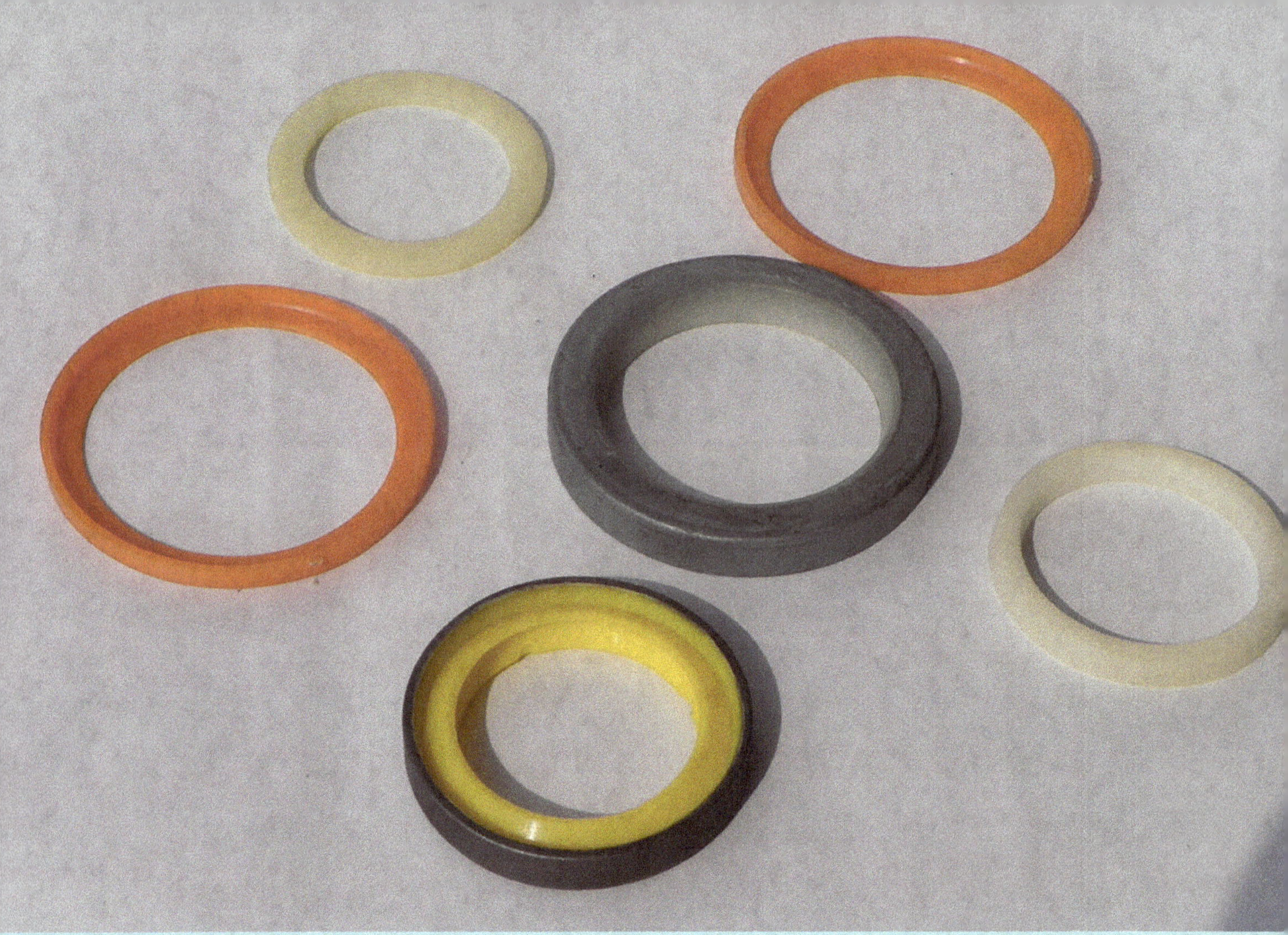

The commission reported that the O-rings sealing the joints on the shuttle's rocket boosters became very brittle in cold temperatures and failed under stress.

**R**ichard Feynman, a member of the commission, made a simple demonstration for the American people using part of an O-ring and a glass of ice water.

CHALLENGER ROCKET BOOSTER

Once the O-ring seals broke on one of the booster rockets on Challenger, flames shot out the side of the rocket and ignited the fuel tank. This led to the disintegration of the whole space shuttle.

The commission noted that the company that had designed the rocket boosters, Morton Thikol, had received warnings about the problem but had ignored them. Some NASA managers were also aware of the problems with the design, but had not taken action.

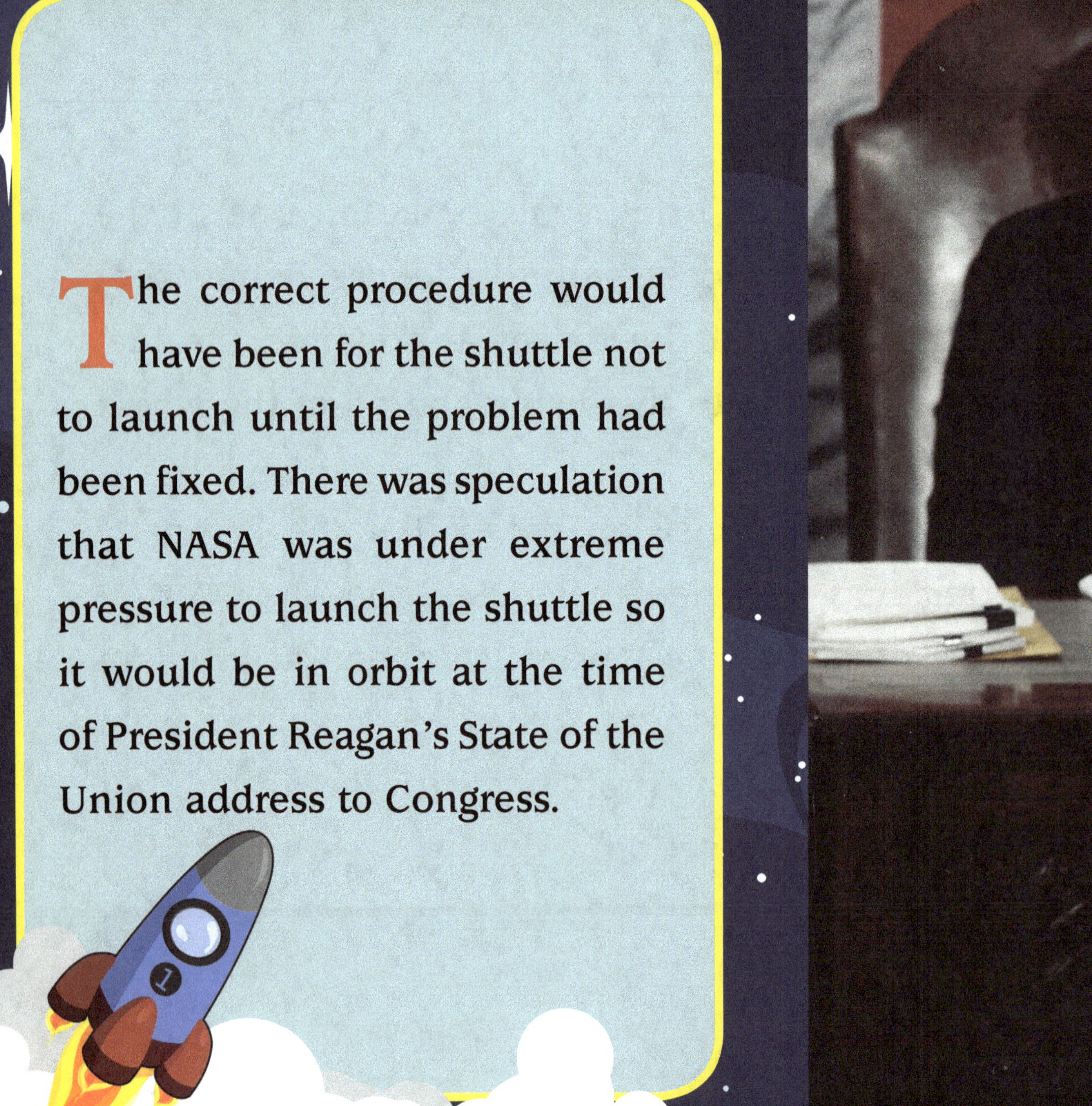

The correct procedure would have been for the shuttle not to launch until the problem had been fixed. There was speculation that NASA was under extreme pressure to launch the shuttle so it would be in orbit at the time of President Reagan's State of the Union address to Congress.

PRESIDENT REAGAN GIVING THE STATE OF
THE UNION ADDRESS TO CONGRESS

Sally Ride, an astronaut member of the commission, made several recommendations to improve decision-making in NASA. Read about her in the Baby Professor book Sally Ride: The First American Woman in Space.

# AFTER THE DISASTER

After the Challenger accident, NASA did not launch further space missions for more than two years. It spent the time addressing problems in several of the shuttle's areas, including the O-rings.

THE CHALLENGER MEMORIAL

SPACE SHUTTLE DISCOVERY

The next shuttle to launch was Discovery, in September, 1988. From then until 2011, the remaining space shuttles carried out many successful missions. These included repairing the Hubble Space Telescope and carrying components to be assembled into the International Space Station. Over nearly thirty years of service, Discovery carried out 39 missions.

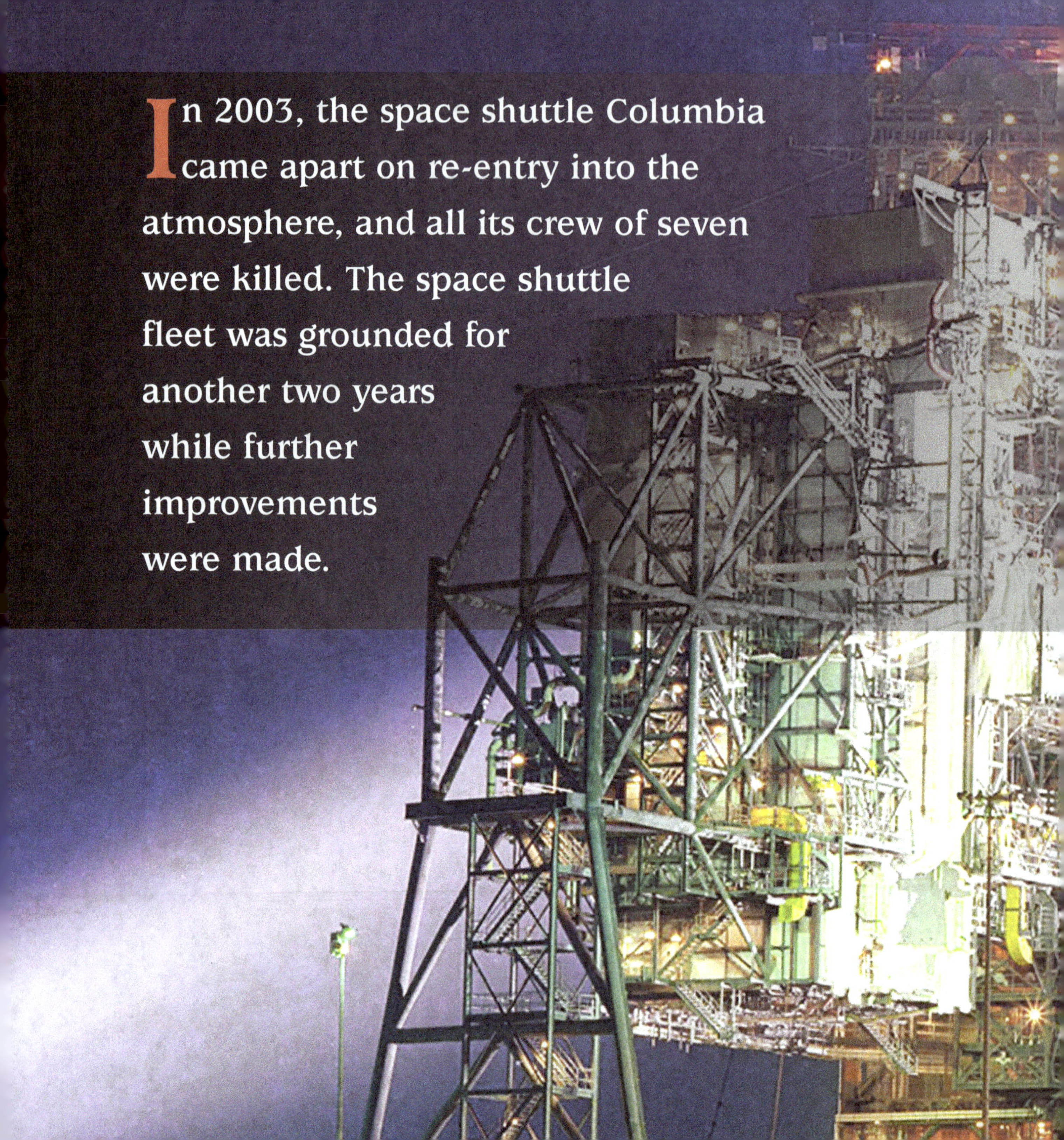
In 2003, the space shuttle Columbia came apart on re-entry into the atmosphere, and all its crew of seven were killed. The space shuttle fleet was grounded for another two years while further improvements were made.

USA
SPACE SHUTTLE COLUMBIA
SITS ON LAUNCH PAD

SPACE SHUTTLE COLUMBIA
United States
USA

In all, five space shuttles carried out 135 missions, with over 355 people taking part in missions—some of them being part of several missions. They were Columbia, Challenger, Discovery, Atlantis, and Endeavor. A sixth space shuttle, Enterprise, was a prototype that flew in the Earth's atmosphere, but never went into space.

After NASA retired the space shuttle fleet in 2011, it has relied on the Russian Soyuz program to carry astronauts to be part of the crew on the International Space Station. Both NASA and several private companies are working on new types of reusable space craft for future space missions.

RUSSIAN SOYUZ

# CHALLENGER FACTS

The Challenger didn't explode. The shuttle was about 46,000 feet up when it was lost in a cloud of smoke and fire, so it looked like an explosion. But the when the O-rings on the booster rocket failed, hot gas poured out of the rocket and ignited the fuel in the fuel tank. This created a huge fireball, without an initial explosion.

The Challenger astronauts did not die immediately. The crew cabin stayed intact, and in fact rose another 20,000 feet in the air before falling back to earth. It hit the ocean about three minutes after the shuttle broke apart, at about 200 miles per hour. The crew probably all lost consciousness when the cabin lost pressure, and probably none of them knew what had happened.

Very few people saw the disaster live, although it was televised live by CNN. Cable news channels were very new in 1986 and had relatively few viewers. The major networks covering the launch cut away to commentators as soon as the disaster happened. Most people saw film of the disaster, with its iconic forked plume of smoke, hours or days after the event.

CHILDREN WATCHING THE CHALLENGER LAUNCHING

Although Christa McAuliffe did not become the first "Teacher in Space", her backup was a former math teacher, Barbara Morgan.

Morgan was a mission specialist on the shuttle Endeavor during a mission in 2007.

RONALD REAGAN

President Reagan postponed the State of the Union address to Congress, the only time so far that it has been postponed. He made a short televised address to the nation that is generally thought to have been one of his best speeches. In his remarks he quoted from a poem by American pilot John McGee Junior, who died during World War II. The poem speaks about slipping "the surly bonds of earth" to "touch the face of God."

More than ten years after the Challenger disaster, large pieces of the spacecraft washed up on a beach in Florida. The two large pieces, one six feet wide and more than 13 feet long, both came from the shuttle's left wing flap.

# DEBRIS OF THE CHALLENGER RECOVERED

The most important parts of the Challenger, including the crew capsule, were retrieved, however most of the spacecraft, the booster rockets, and the fuel tank are still in the Atlantic Ocean. Five thousand pieces of debris, weighing together over 250,000 pounds, are stored in two abandoned missile silos.

# YEARNING FOR OUTER SPACE

Traveling in space is a great project for humanity, not just for one country or one mission crew. Several groups are already trying to solve all the life-threatening challenges of setting up and living in a human colony on Mars or on our Moon. Others are looking even further away, to moons of the gas giant planets Jupiter and Saturn that might even support life!

APOLLO 17 ON THE MOON

Imagine what it would be like to travel in space! Read Baby Professor books like *A Space Ride to Saturn!* to learn more.

Visit
BABY PROFESSOR
EDUCATION KIDS
www.BabyProfessorBooks.com
to download Free Baby Professor eBooks
and view our catalog of new and exciting
Children's Books